ALBERTO GINASTERA

SONATINA

for Harp

T0087299

BOOSEY & HAWKES

DISTRIBUTED BY
HAL•LEONARD®
7777 W. BLUEMOUND RD. P.O. BOX 13819 MILWAUKEE, WI 53213

www.boosey.com
www.halleonard.com

In his early years Alberto Ginastera composed several works that were premièred with considerable success, but did not find their way into his official work catalogue. These include the present Sonatina for solo harp from the year 1938. It was given its first performance by Inés Sebastiani in Buenos Aires on 26 June 1939, and was shortly afterwards awarded the Premio Municipal de Música. Despite this success, Ginastera did not make any effort to have the work published, as he was meanwhile occupied with other, more ambitious projects. But nor did he distance himself completely from it. Not only did he show his early Sonatina to several interested harpists, but he explicitly reworked material from its third movement in the Finale of his Harp Concerto op. 25 (1956-65). Moreover, in his final years Ginastera undertook a series of corrections and annotations in a manuscript copy in his possession, which suggests that he may have been considering a retrospective publication of the score. Copies of it had in any case long been circulating among musicians, and "inofficial" performances of the Sonatina were not uncommon.

The present edition of this unpretentious and beautifully crafted early work draws on two primary sources preserved in the composer's archives in the Paul Sacher Foundation: a fair copy, possibly in Ginastera's own hand, and a photocopy of the annotated score mentioned above. However, the modifications found in the latter, often intended to make the work more convenient to perform, are too sketchily and cursorily notated to enable us to reconstruct from it any reliable "revised edition". For this reason, they were not incorporated in the present edition, which is based solely on the musical text of 1938. A further editorial decision was made regarding the rather inconsistent use of dynamic and articulation markings in the manuscript sources. Where these markings diverge in parallel passages for no recognizable reason, they were judiciously brought into line. But where both primary sources demonstrate the same divergences in such parallel passages, no attempt was made to harmonize them.

—Felix Meyer
Paul Sacher Foundation

*Special thanks to Clinton F. Nieweg,
and Ursula Holliger*

al Maestro Augusto Sebastiani

SONATINA
for Harp

I. PRELUDIO

Alberto Ginastera
(1938)

Allegro

979-0-051-09844-6

First printing 2020

II. ARIA

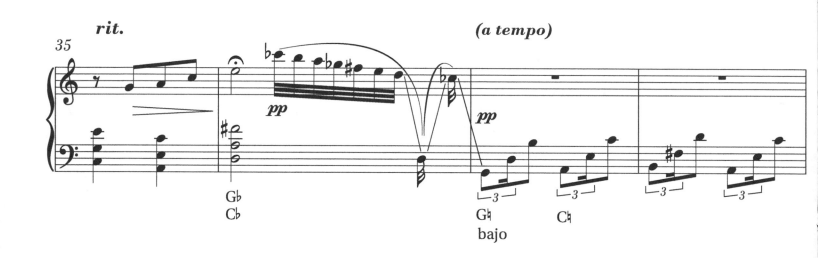

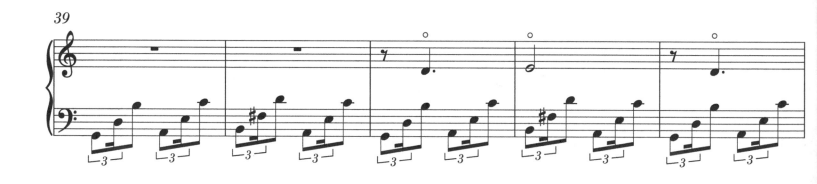

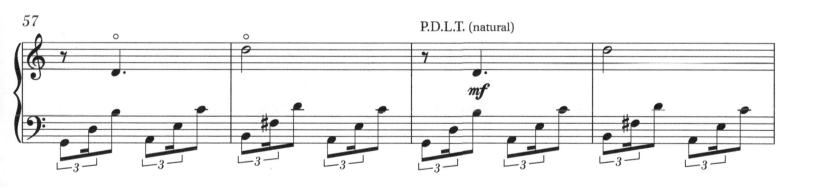

III. Toccata

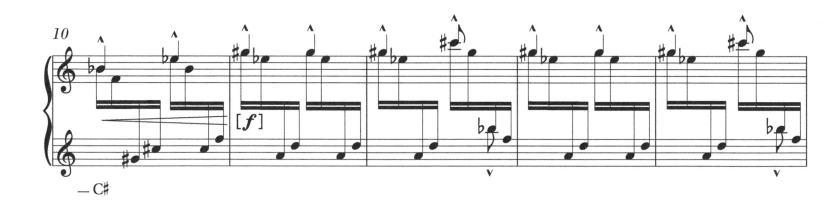

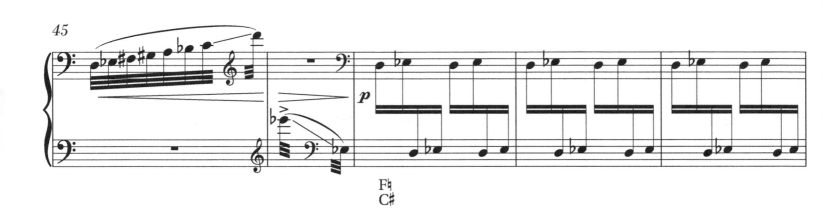

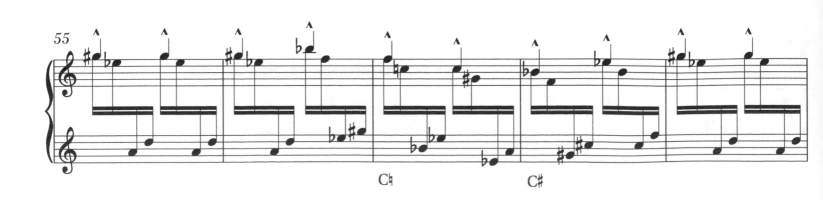

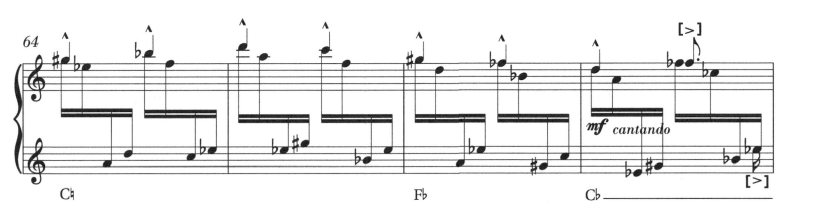

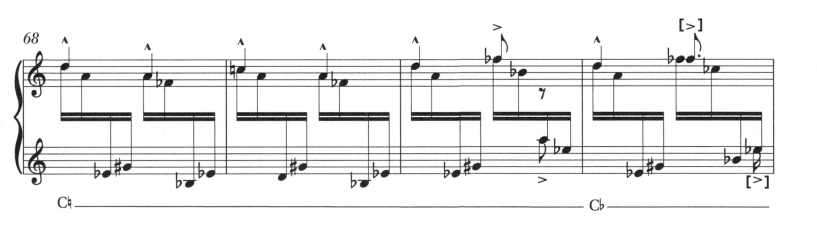

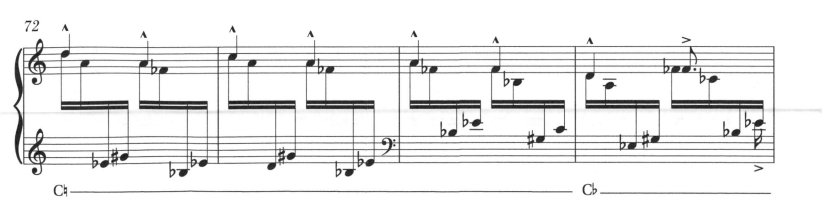

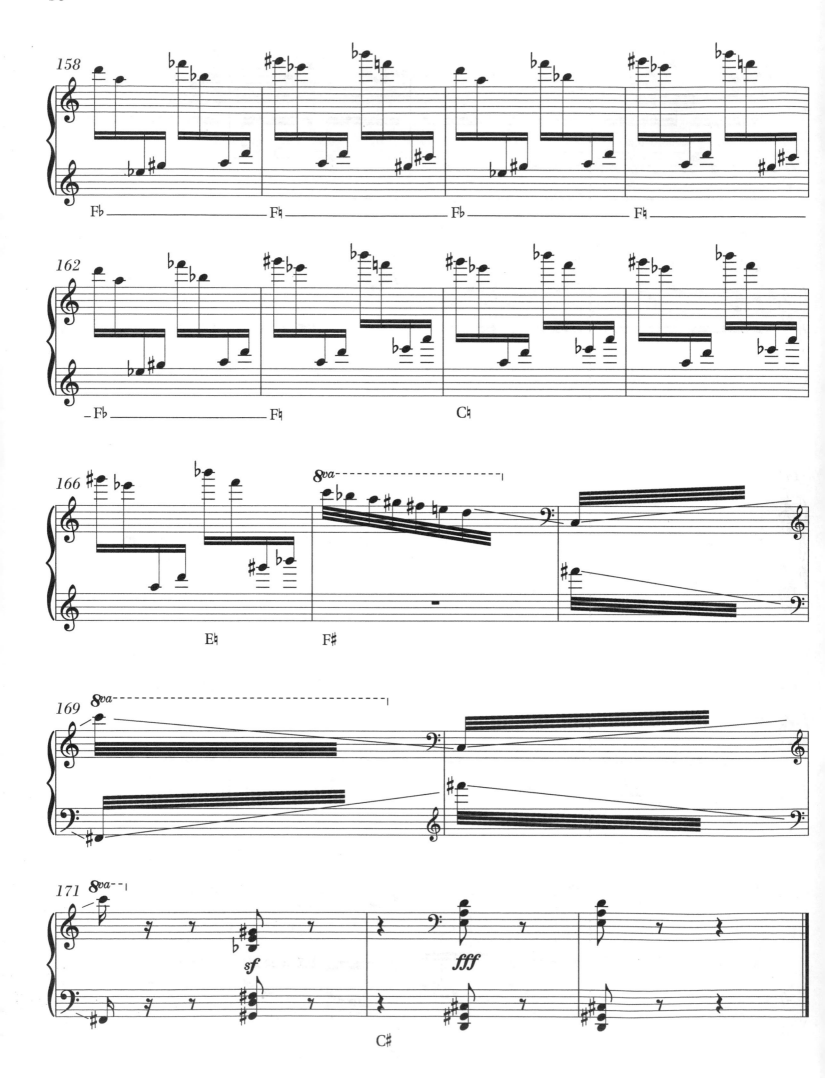